ZAPEDELIC
COLORING BOOK

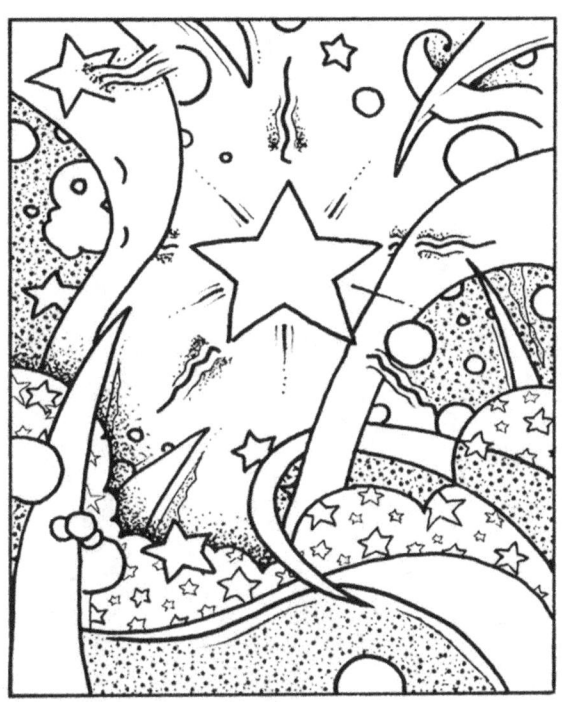

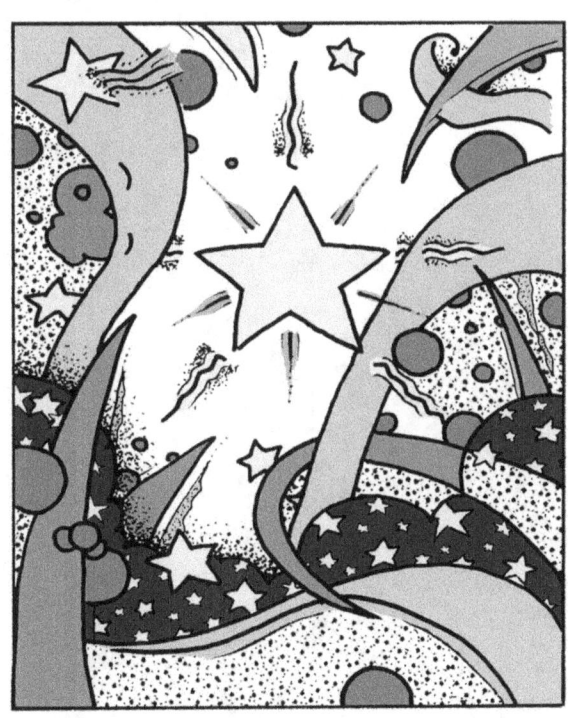

13 READY-TO-COLOR PSYCHEDELIC DRAWINGS!

DESIGNED AND PUBLISHED BY BOB ANDROVICH

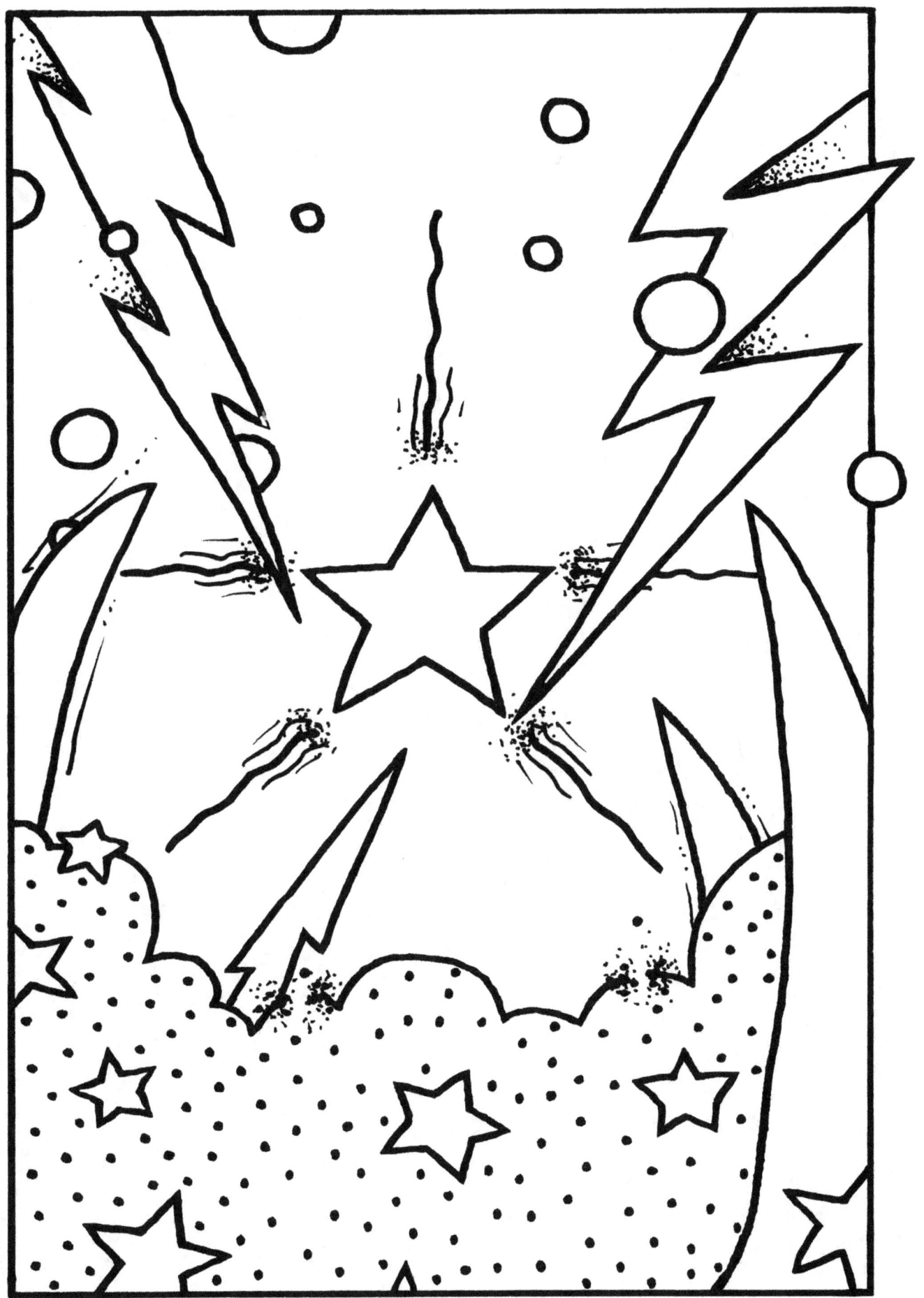

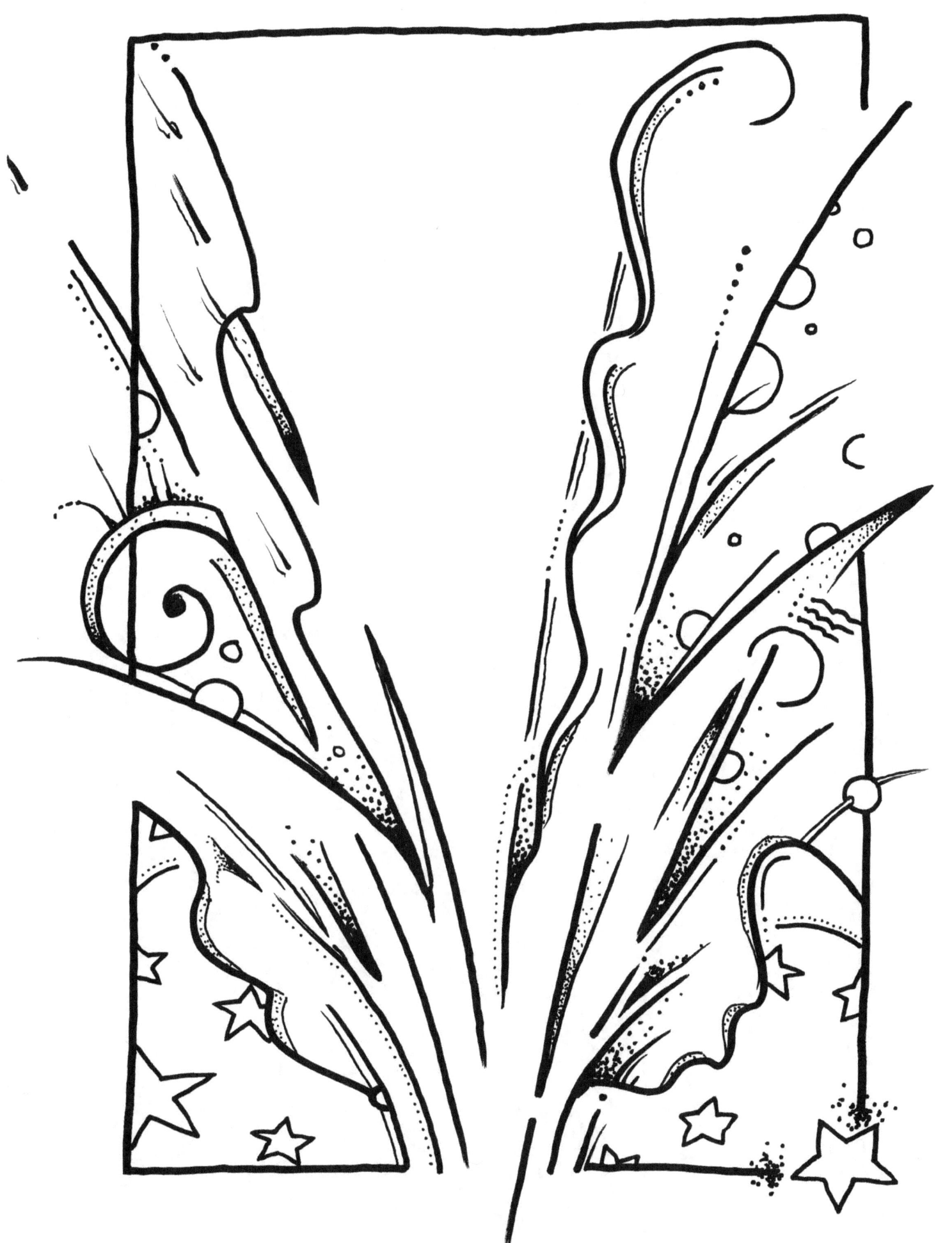

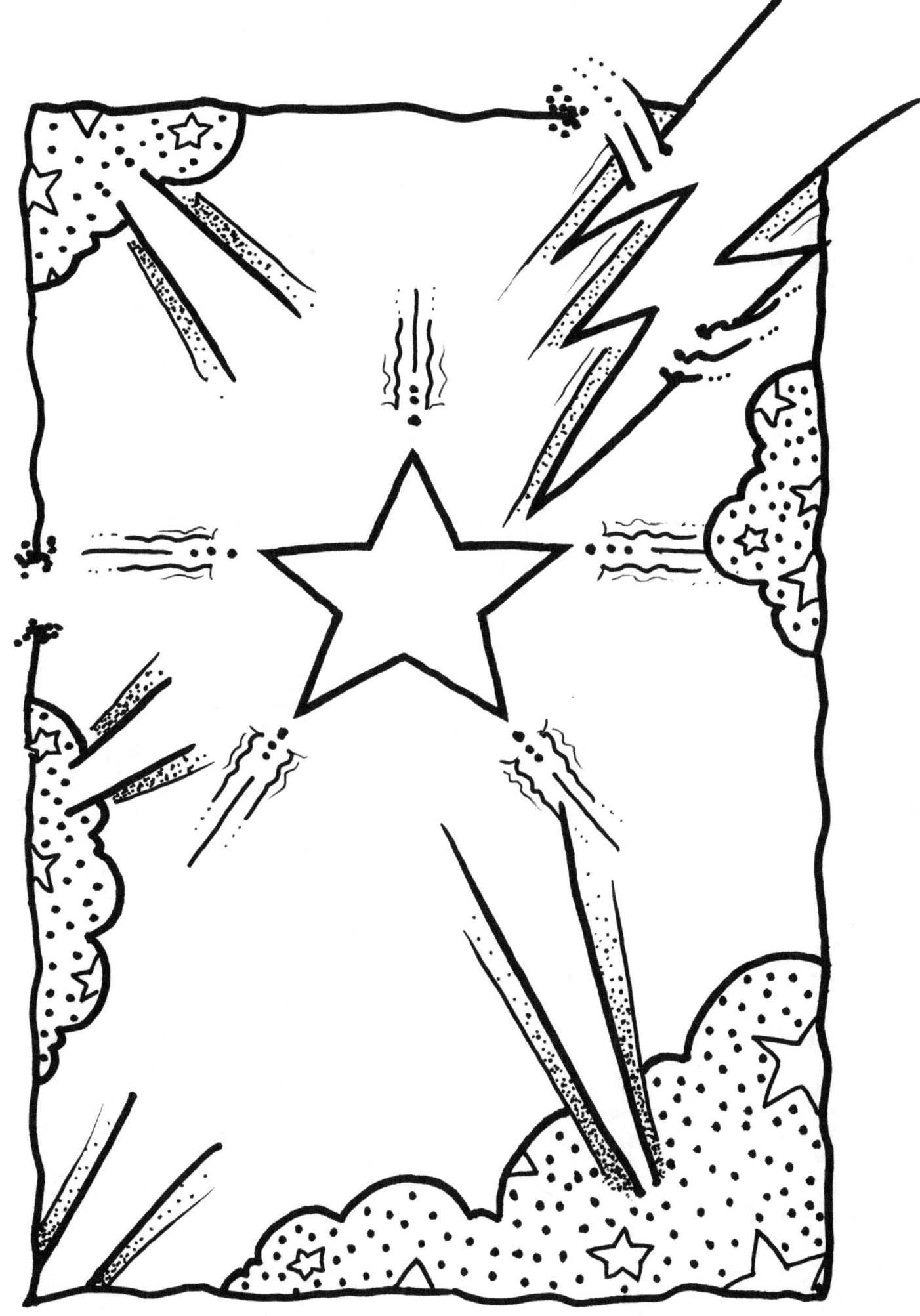

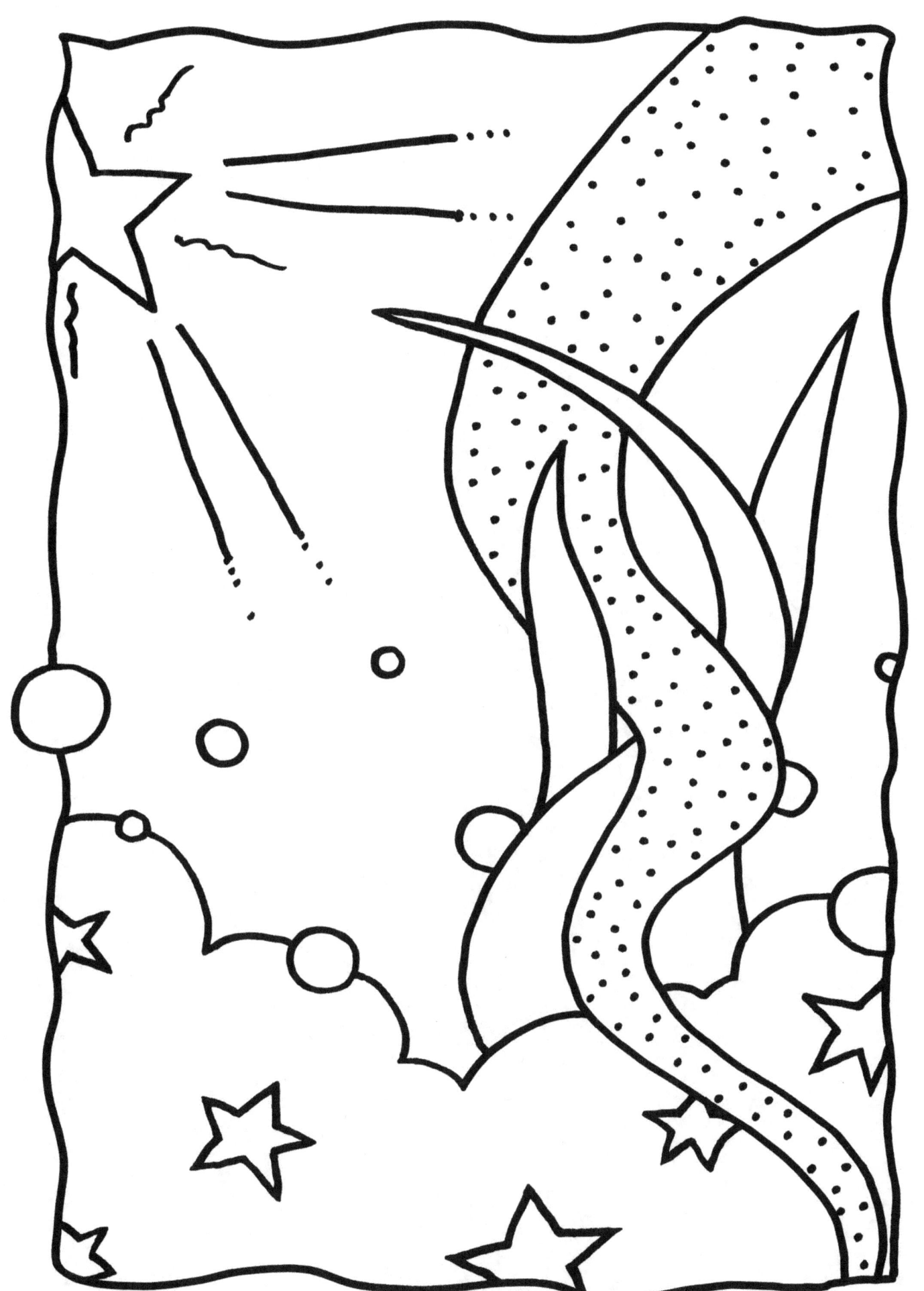

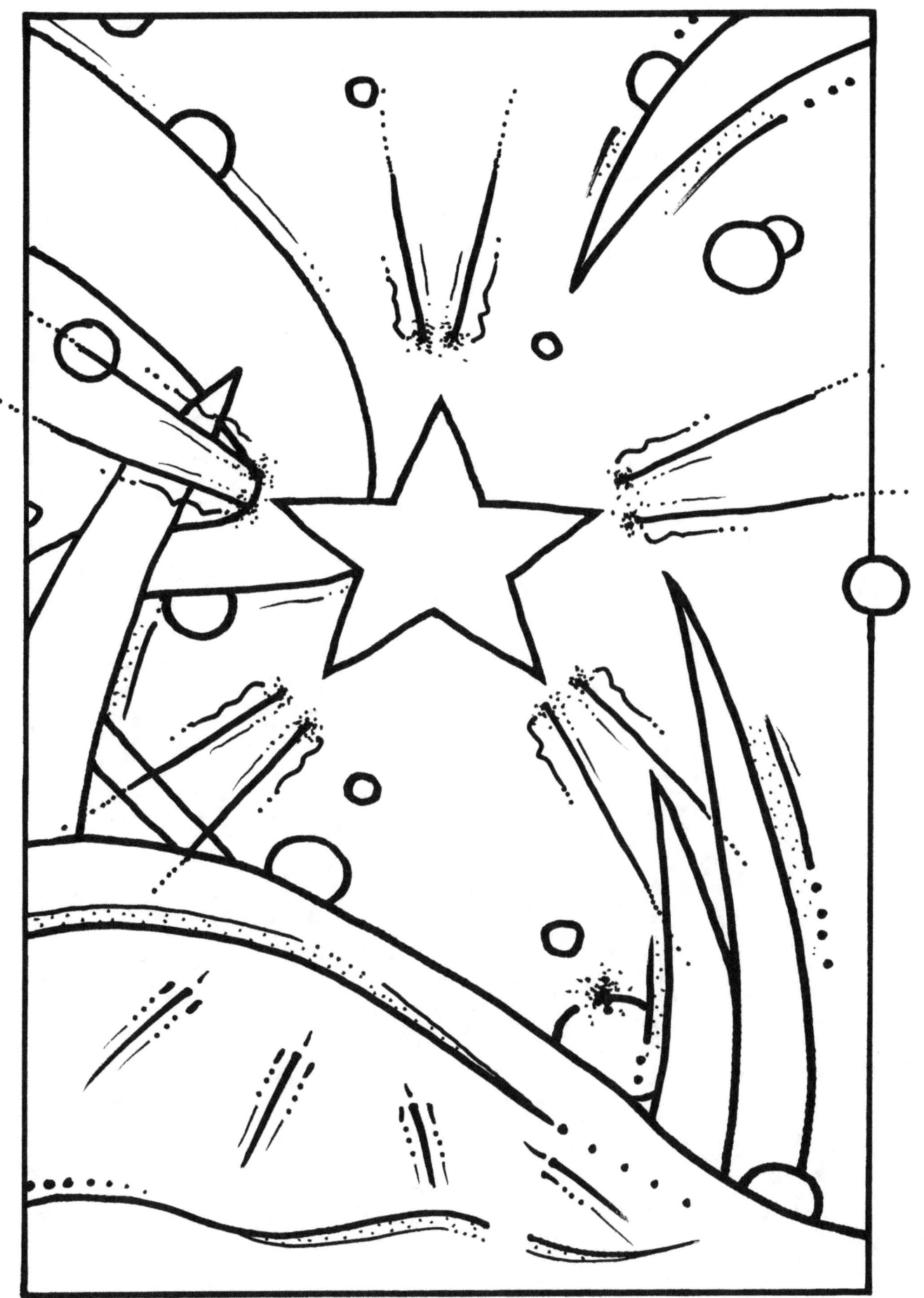

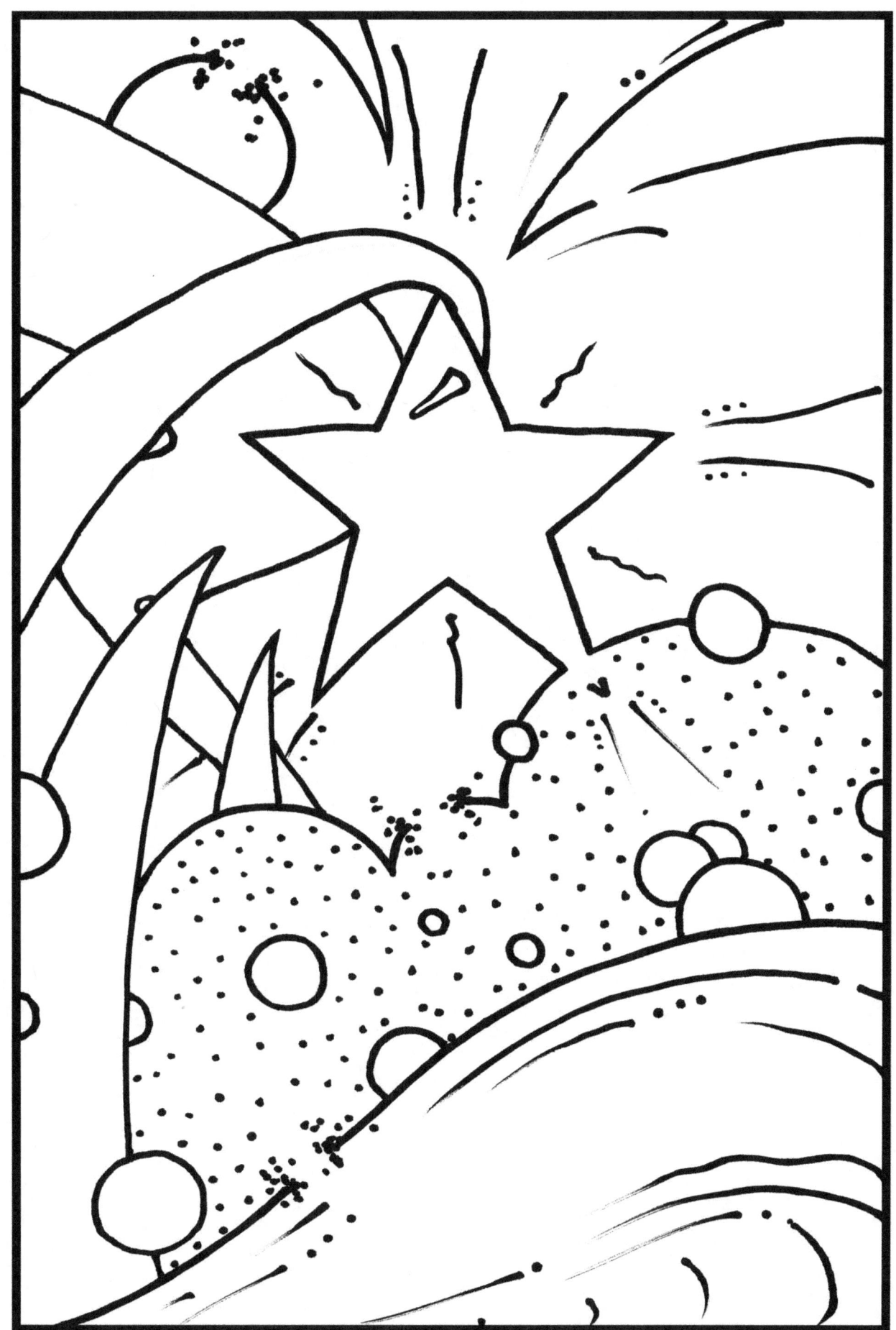

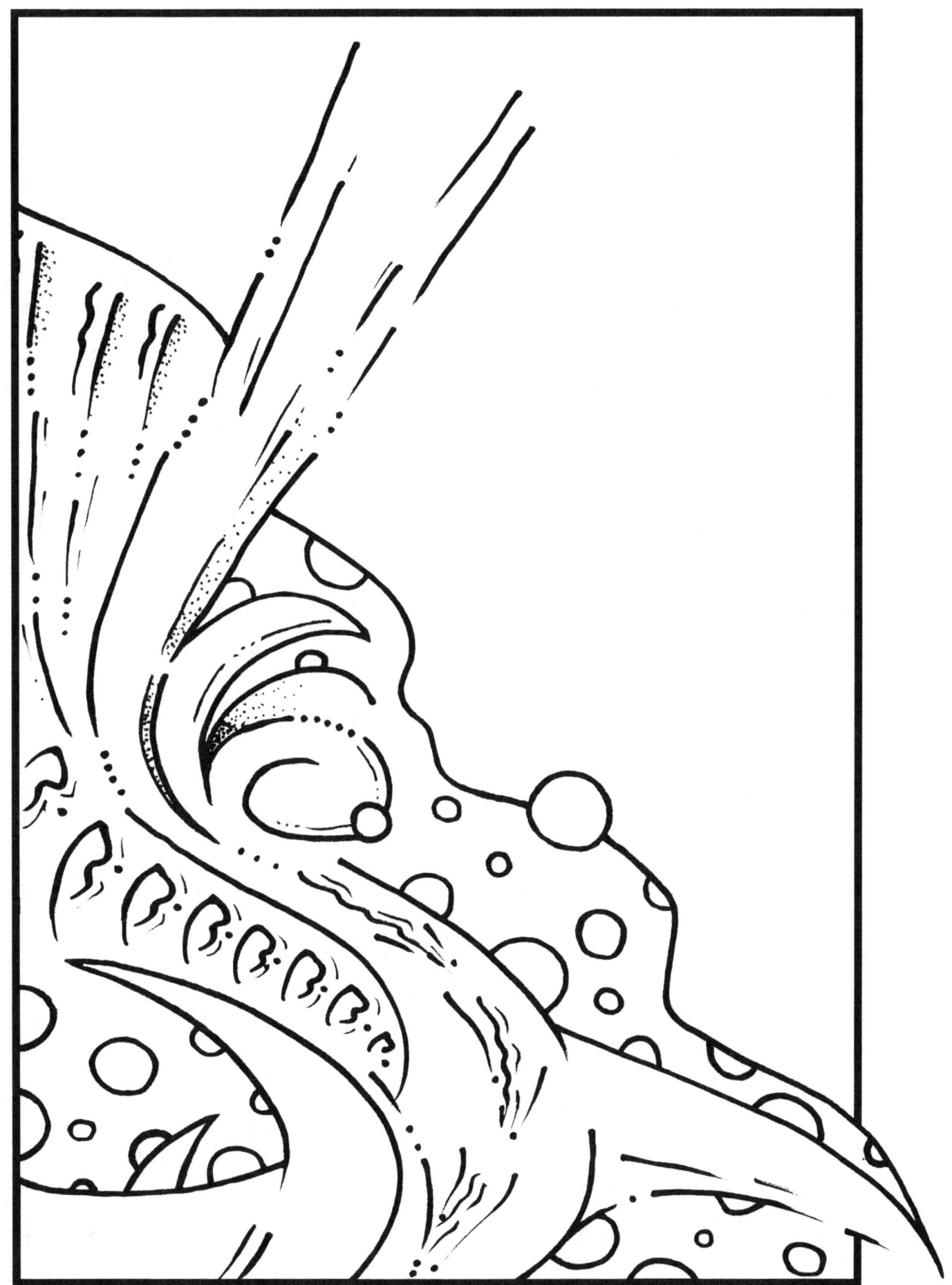

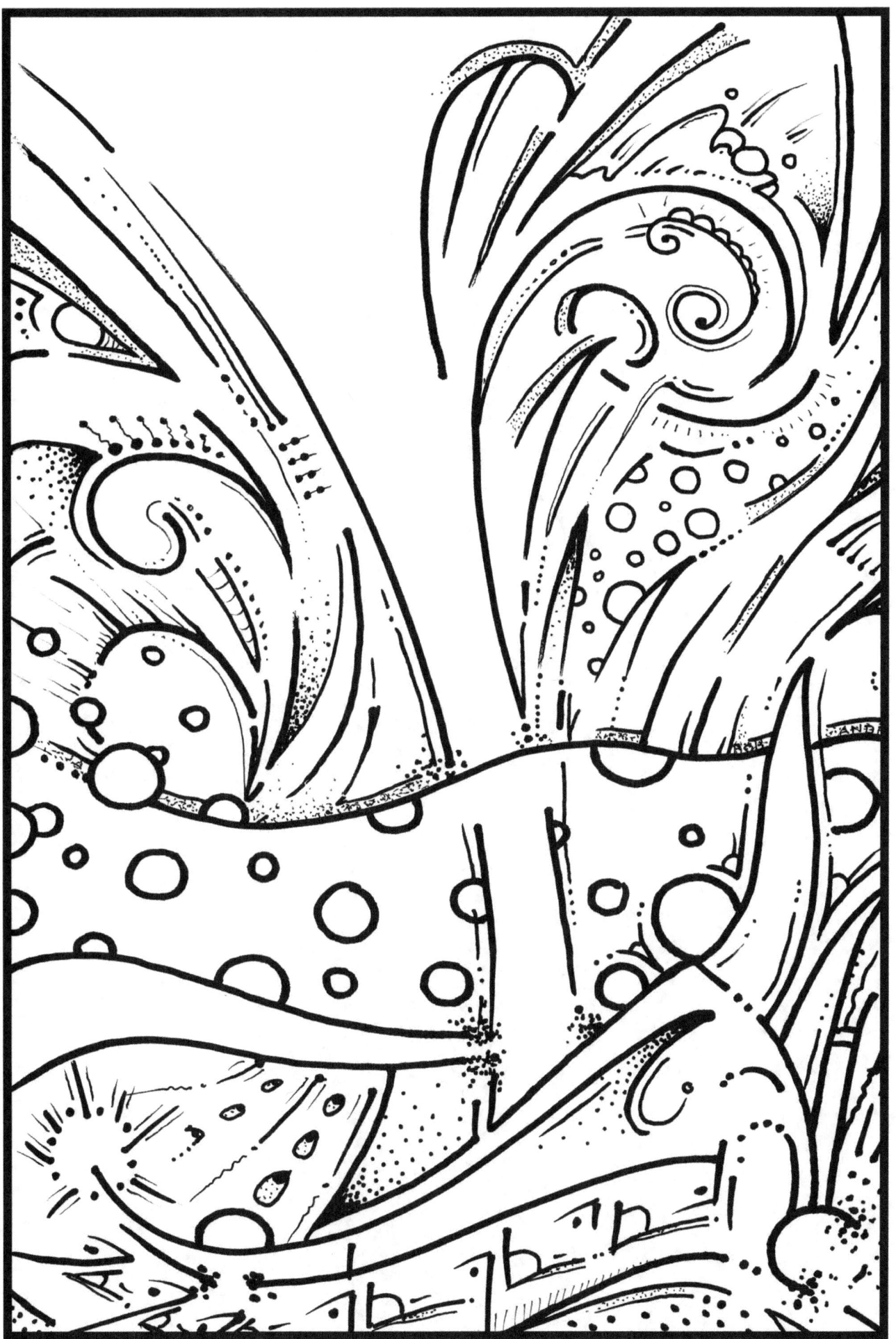

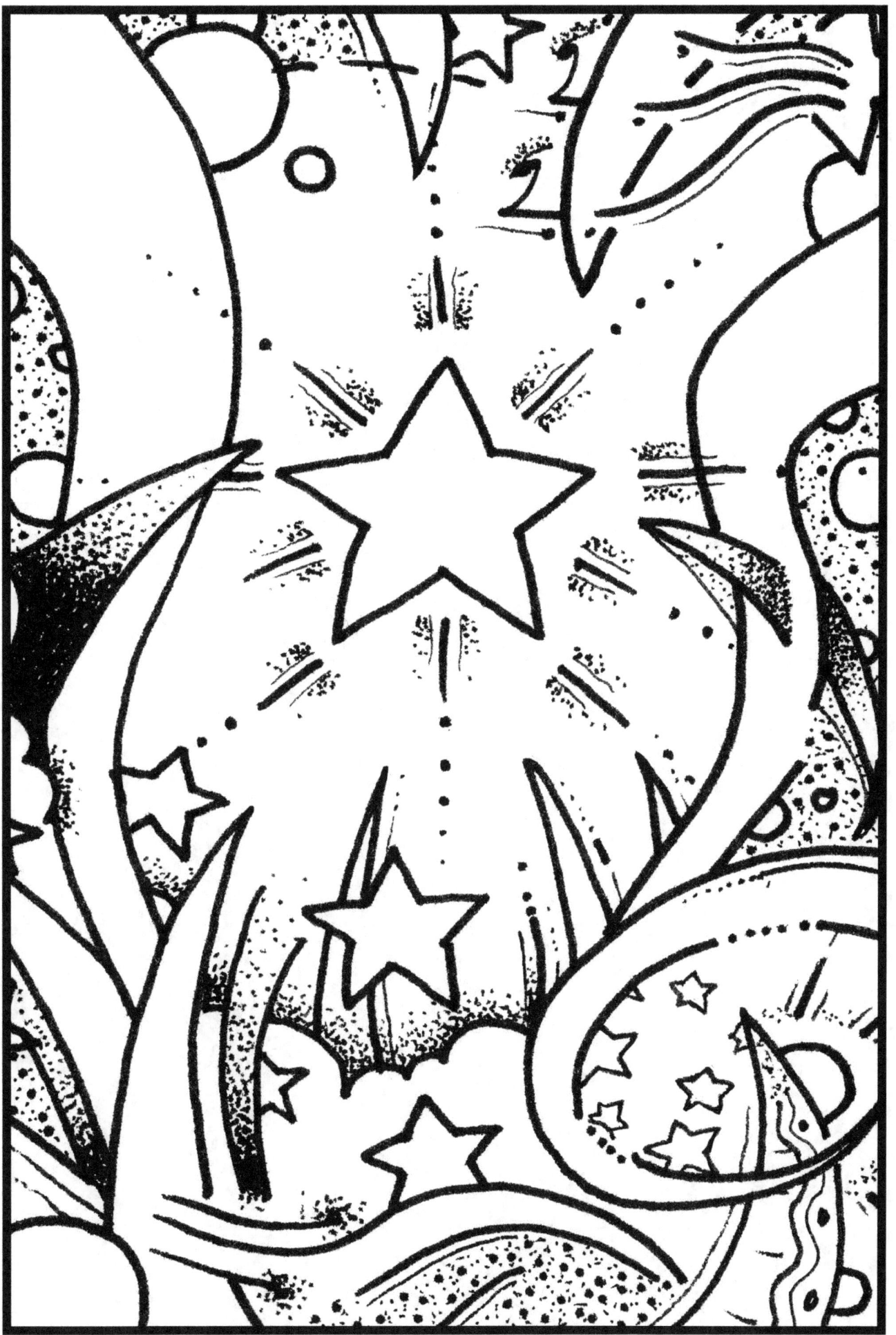

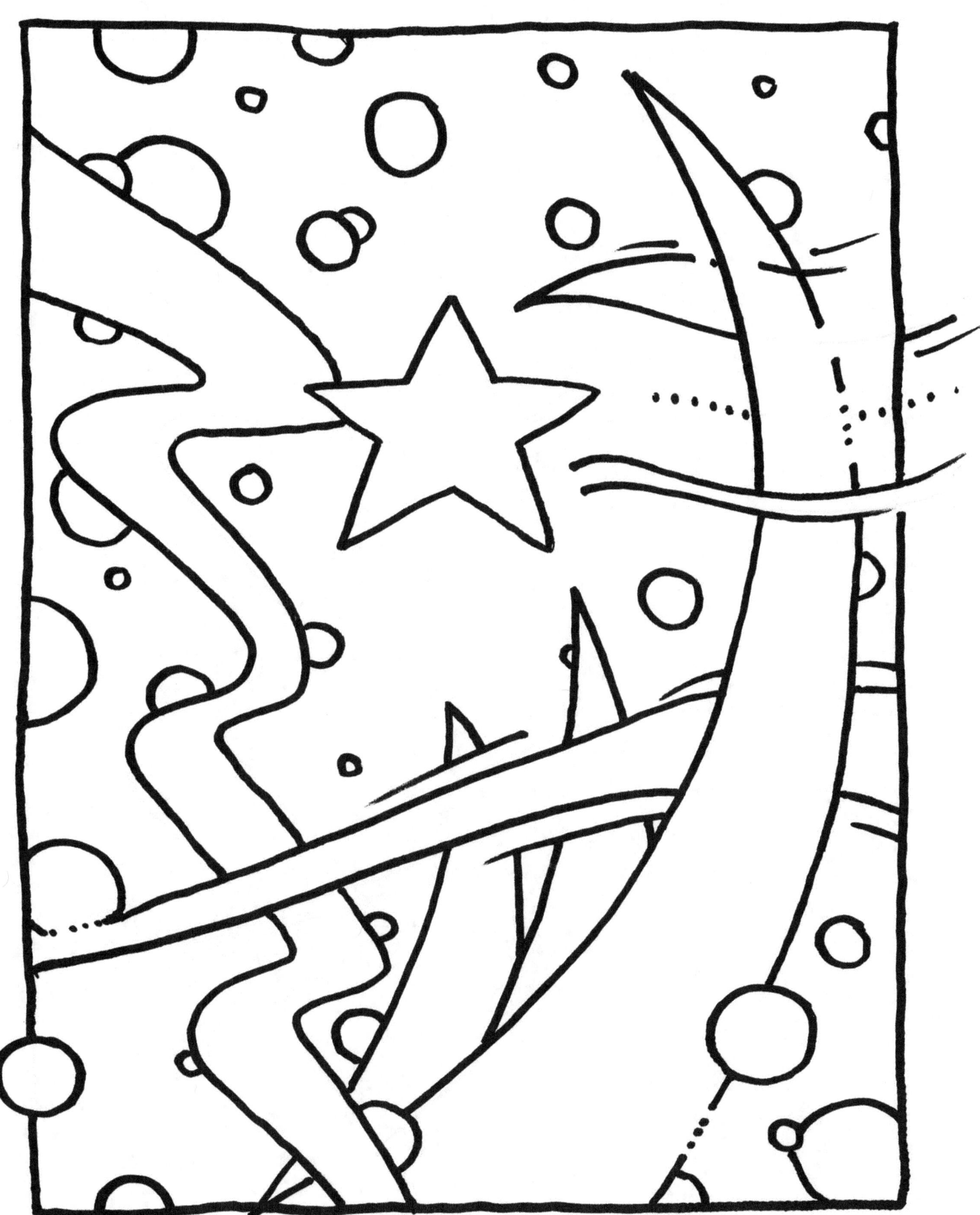

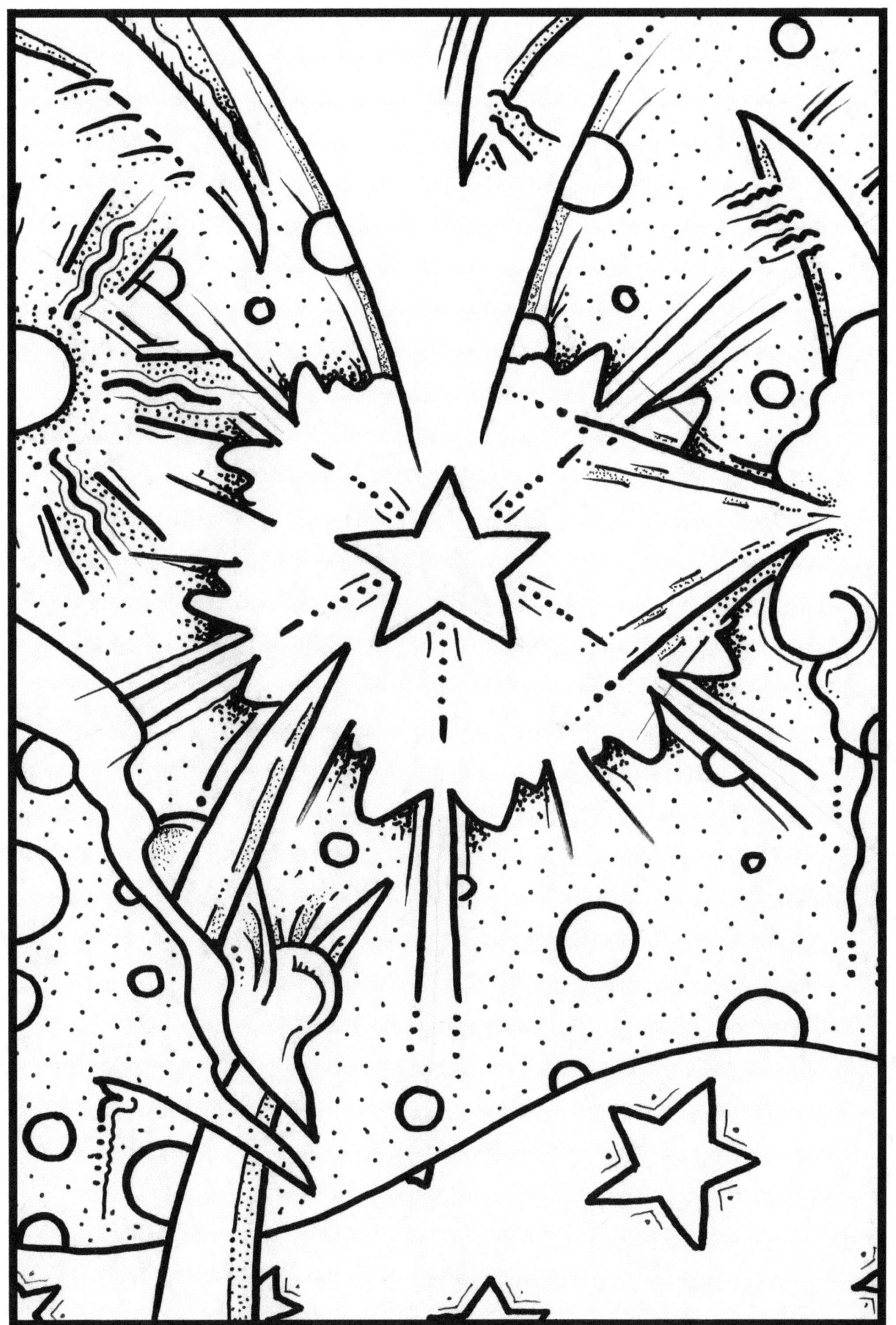

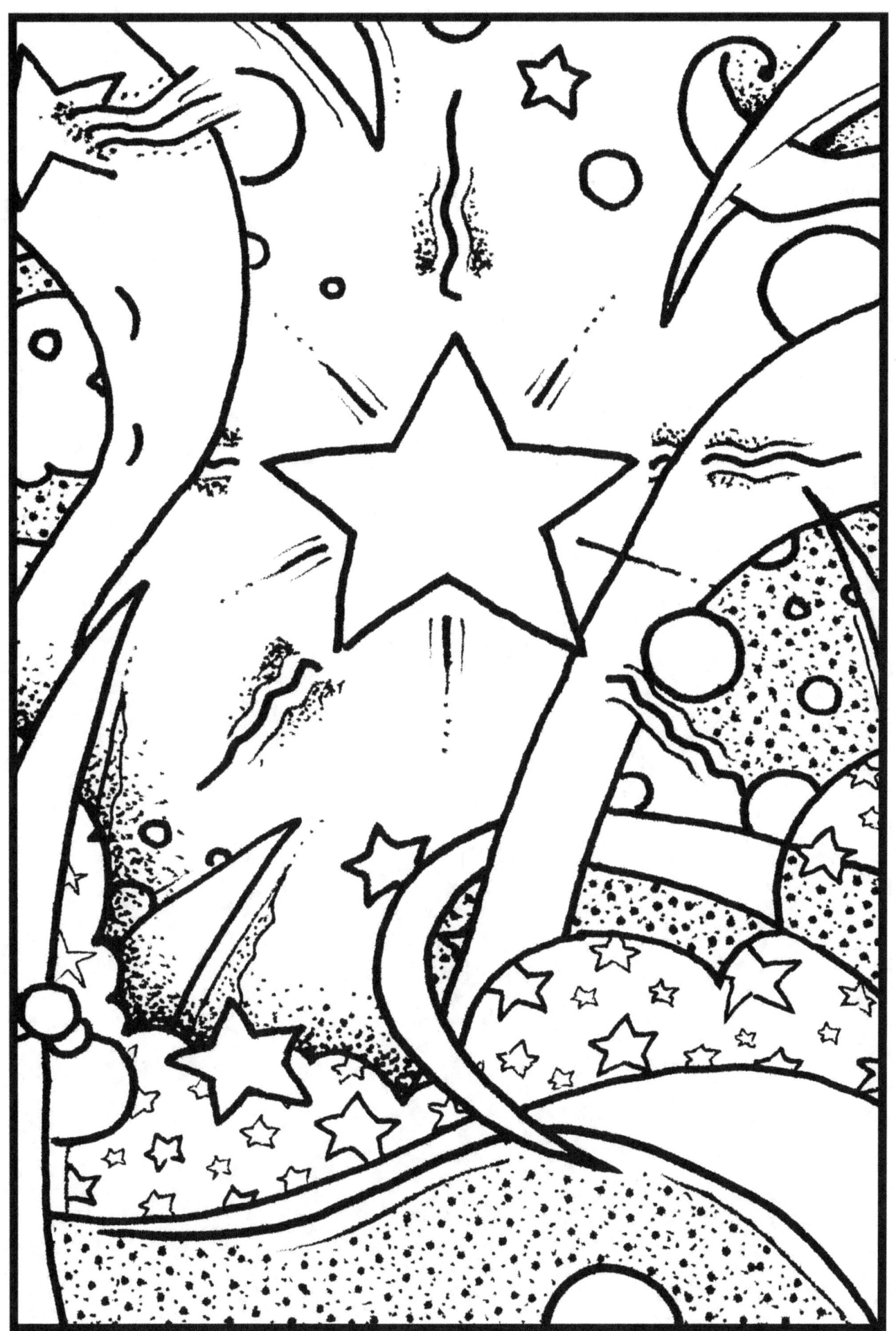

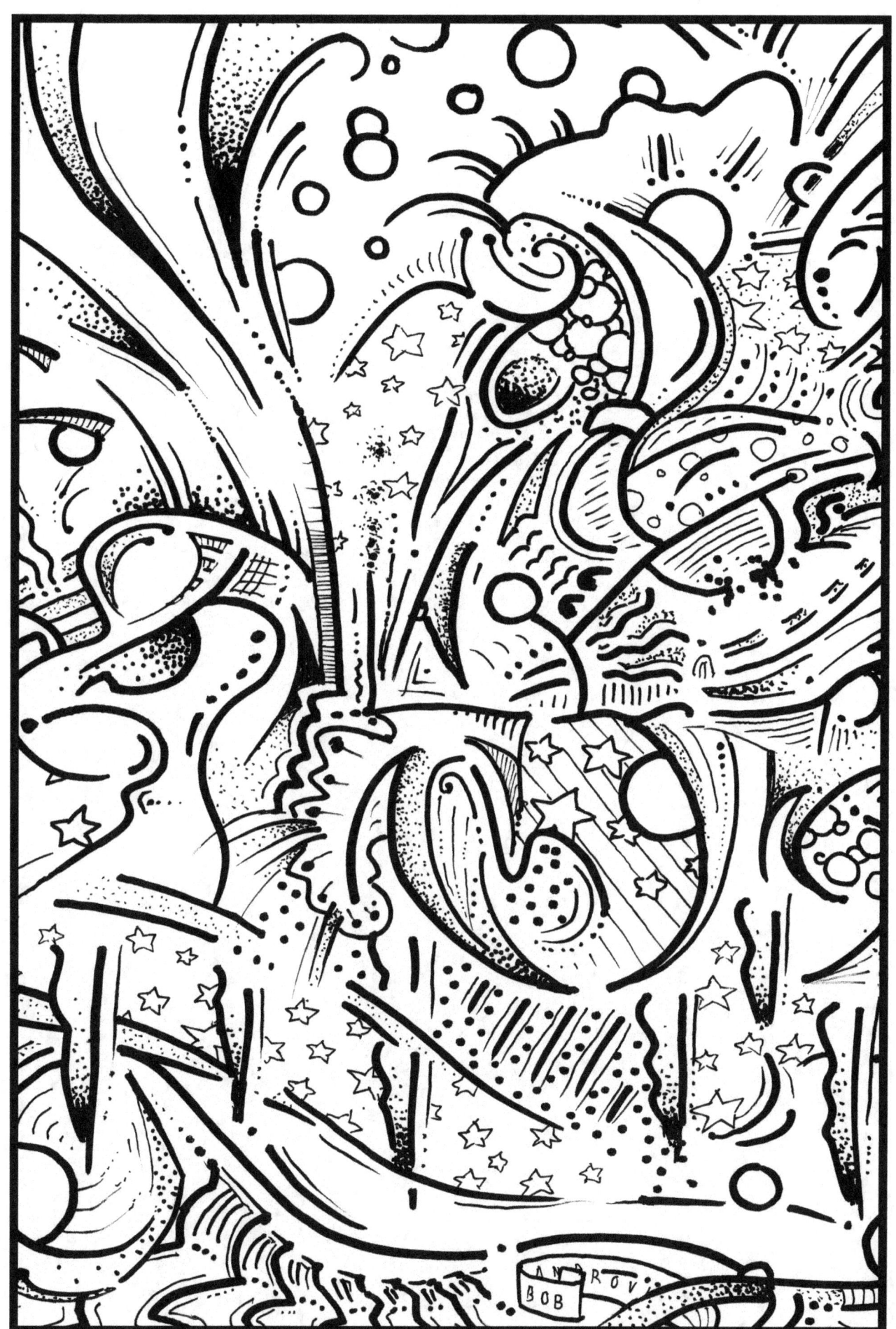

www.ingramcontent.com/pod-product-compliance
Lightning Source LLC
Chambersburg PA
CBHW060009230526
45472CB00008B/2011